30 Day D

MW01172295

Worsnip

Rev. Dr. Dennis Snyder

DEDICATION

To my wife of 52 years who has been a God send and the best thing that has happened to me, outside of Trusting Jesus Christ as my Lord and Savior.

She has helped me to grow in my faith and challenged me to be the husband, father and man that God wants me to be. Without her influence I doubt that I would be the man that I am. She has been such a help as we served together in the ministry God has put us in.

WHY HAVE A DAILY
DEVOTION/PRAYER TIME

Having a daily devotional time is important for you as a believer in Christ Jesus and His shed blood. It can help you to build a closer relationship with God. By setting aside time each day to read the Bible, pray, and reflect on your faith, you can deepen your understanding of God's word and grow in your spiritual journey. This daily practice can also help you to stay focused on your faith and to maintain a sense of peace and purpose in your life, even during difficult times.

Having a daily devotional time can also help you to stay accountable to yourself and to God. By committing to a regular practice of prayer and study, you can stay focused on your faith and avoid getting sidetracked by the distractions of daily life. This can help you to live more intentionally and to make choices that align with your biblical values and beliefs.

Having a daily time of prayer can be important for you because it can help you to connect with God and to communicate your worship, thoughts, feelings, and needs. By establishing a routine of prayer, you can develop a sense of discipline in your spiritual life and create a regular opportunity to express gratitude, seek guidance, and ask for forgiveness.

Prayer can also provide comfort and strength during difficult times. By taking time to pray each day, you can find solace in your faith and feel more connected to your Lord. This can provide a sense of peace and calmness in the midst of stress and uncertainty.

Having a daily time of prayer can also help you to cultivate a deeper relationship with God. By making prayer a regular part of your routine, you can develop a more intimate and personal connection with your faith and your God. This can lead to a greater sense of purpose and meaning in your life, as well as a greater understanding of your values and beliefs.

Spend the next 30 days reading this short devotional and praying the daily prayer out loud. This will help you to get in the habit of meeting and talking to God on a regular daily basis.

The repetition in these daily readings is intentional. They are meant to cement into our hearts the truth of God's Word. This will help you to live out these truths in your daily living.

Get in the daily habit of reading and talking to your Heavenly Father. Above all, keep your focus on the King of kings and Lord of lords, Jesus Christ.

Revelation 5:11-14

11. Then I looked, and I heard the voice of many angels around the throne, the living creatures, and the elders; and the number of them was ten thousand times ten thousand, and thousands of thousands, 12. saying with a loud voice:

> *"Worthy is the Lamb who was slain*
> *To receive power and riches and wisdom,*
> *And strength and honor and glory and blessing!"*

13. And every creature which is in heaven and on the earth and under the earth and such as are in the sea, and all that are in them, I heard saying:

> *"Blessing and honor and glory and power*
> *Be to Him who sits on the throne,*
> *And to the Lamb, forever and ever!"*

14. Then the four living creatures said, "Amen!" And the twenty-four elders fell down and worshiped Him who lives forever and ever.

DAY ONE

"Therefore, I urge you, brothers and sisters, in view of God's mercy, to offer your bodies as a living sacrifice, holy and pleasing to God—this is your true and proper worship." - Romans 12:1

Romans 12:1 is a powerful verse that calls believers to offer their bodies as living sacrifices to God. The passage begins with the word "Therefore," which indicates that the apostle Paul is building on the ideas he has presented throughout the previous chapters. In Romans 1-11, Paul has explained the gospel of Jesus Christ and the incredible love and mercy that God has shown to humanity. He has emphasized that salvation is a free gift of grace, and that it is available to all who believe in Jesus Christ.

In Romans 12:1, Paul urges believers to respond to God's mercy by offering their bodies as living sacrifices. This means that we are to give ourselves completely to God, holding nothing back. We are to surrender our desires, our plans, and our ambitions to Him, and allow Him to use us as He sees fit.

Paul emphasizes that this kind of sacrifice is "holy and pleasing to God." In other words, when we offer ourselves to God in this way, we are worshiping Him and demonstrating our love and devotion to Him. This is the kind of worship that God desires from His people - not just singing songs or attending church services, but a complete surrender of our lives to Him.

The verse closes with the words, "This is your true and proper worship." This is a reminder that true worship is not just about external rituals or practices, but about the condition of our hearts. When we offer ourselves as living sacrifices to God, we are worshiping Him in spirit and in truth, and living out the gospel message in our daily lives.

Prayer:

Father, I come to You today, humbled by Your mercy and grace. I am grateful for the gift of salvation that You have given me through Your Son, Jesus Christ. I thank You that You have called me to be a living sacrifice, holy and pleasing to You.

Lord, I offer myself to You today. I surrender my desires, my plans, and my ambitions to You. I ask that You would use me as You see fit, for Your glory and Your purposes. Help me to live my life in a way that is pleasing to You, and to be a witness to Your love and grace.

I pray that You would transform me by renewing my mind. Help me to think and act in a way that is consistent with Your will and Your Word. Give me the strength and courage to resist the temptations of this world, and to follow You wholeheartedly.

Lord, I ask that You would fill me with Your Holy Spirit, and empower me to live a life that is worthy of the gospel. Help me to love others as You have loved me, and to serve them with humility and compassion.

Thank You, God, for Your incredible love and mercy. I pray that my life would be a living sacrifice, holy and pleasing to You. May all that I do bring honor and glory to Your name.

In Jesus' name I pray,
Amen.

DAY TWO

"Let us worship and bow down; let us kneel before the Lord our Maker." -
Psalm 95:6

Psalm 95:6 is a call to worship and bow down before the Lord our Maker.
The verse begins with the word "Oh," indicating a sense of urgency and
enthusiasm for worship. The psalmist is inviting all people to join in
worshiping the Lord and acknowledging His sovereignty over all creation.

The verse emphasizes the importance of humility and reverence in worship.
To bow down before the Lord is a physical expression of submission and
respect, acknowledging that He is greater than us and worthy of our
worship. It is also a reminder that we are not in control, but that God is the
one who holds all power and authority.

The phrase "our Maker" emphasizes the fact that God is the one who
created us and sustains us. He is not just a distant deity, but a personal God
who cares for His people and desires to be in relationship with them.

Psalm 95:6 is a reminder that worship is not just a ritual or a duty, but a
heartfelt response to God's love and grace. It is an opportunity to express
our gratitude and adoration for all that He has done for us, and to deepen
our relationship with Him.

In summary, Psalm 95:6 is a call to worship and bow down before the Lord
our Maker with humility and reverence. It reminds us of God's sovereignty,
His care for us, and the importance of worship as a response to His love
and grace.

Prayer:

*Dear God, as I come before You today, I am filled with a sense of awe and
reverence for Your greatness. You are the Creator of the universe, the
Maker of all things, and the One who sustains us day by day. I bow down
before You in humility and gratitude, acknowledging Your sovereignty over
all creation.*

Lord, I thank You for Your love and grace, which have been poured out on me in abundance. You have blessed me with so many good things, and I am grateful for Your provision and care. Help me to never take Your blessings for granted, but to always be mindful of Your goodness and mercy.

As I worship You today, I ask that You would fill me with Your Holy Spirit. Help me to worship You in spirit and in truth, with all of my heart, soul, mind, and strength. May my worship be a reflection of my love for You, and a testimony to Your greatness and power.

Lord, I pray that You would deepen my relationship with You through worship. Help me to draw closer to You, to know You more intimately, and to experience Your presence in my life. May my worship be a catalyst for transformation, as You renew my mind and transform me into the image of Your Son.

Thank You, God, for the privilege of worshiping You. May all that I do bring honor and glory to Your name, and may my life be a living sacrifice, holy and pleasing to You.

In Jesus' name I pray, Amen.

DAY THREE

"But the hour is coming, and now is, when the true worshipers will worship the Father in spirit and truth; for the Father is seeking such to worship Him." - John 4:23

John 4:23 is a powerful verse that speaks to the heart of true worship. In this passage, Jesus is speaking to a Samaritan woman at a well, and He tells her that the time is coming when true worshipers will worship the Father in spirit and truth. He emphasizes that God is seeking such worshipers, and that those who worship Him must do so in spirit and truth.

The phrase "in spirit" refers to the innermost part of our being, our heart and soul. True worship is not just a matter of outward actions or rituals, but a matter of the heart. It is a response to God's love and grace, and a reflection of our love for Him.

The phrase "in truth" emphasizes the importance of worshiping God according to His Word and His will. True worship is not just a matter of personal preference or cultural tradition, but a matter of aligning our hearts and minds with God's truth.

John 4:23 is a call to true worship, emphasizing the importance of worshiping God in spirit and truth. It reminds us that worship is not just a matter of outward actions or cultural tradition, but a matter of the heart and our alignment with God's truth. It is a call to worship God with all of our being, in spirit and in truth, and to seek His will in all that we do.

Prayer:

Dear God,

As I come before You today, I am reminded of Your call to true worship. You desire that I worship You in spirit and in truth, with all of my heart, soul, mind, and strength.

Lord, I ask that You would fill me with Your Holy Spirit, and help me to worship You with my whole being. May my worship be a reflection of my love for You, and a response to Your love and grace.

As I worship You, I ask that You would help me to align my heart and mind with Your truth. Guide me by Your Word and Your Spirit, and help me to worship You in a way that is pleasing to You.

Lord, I pray that You would deepen my relationship with You through worship. Help me to draw closer to You, to know You more intimately, and to experience Your presence in my life. May my worship be a catalyst for transformation, as You renew my mind and transform me into the image of Your Son.

Thank You, God, for the privilege of worshiping You. May all that I do bring honor and glory to Your name, and may my life be a living sacrifice, holy and pleasing to You.

In Jesus' name I pray, Amen.

DAY FOUR

"Give unto the Lord the glory due to His name; worship the Lord in the beauty of holiness." - Psalm 29:2

Psalm 29:2 is a powerful verse that emphasizes the importance of giving glory to God. The psalmist calls on the heavenly beings to ascribe glory to the Lord and to worship Him in the beauty of holiness. The phrase "give unto the Lord" means to attribute or give credit to God for His greatness and power.

The verse emphasizes that God is worthy of our worship and praise. He is the Creator of the universe, the King of kings and Lord of lords, and the One who holds all power and authority. He is holy and righteous, and His glory is beyond measure.

The phrase "worship the Lord in the beauty of holiness" emphasizes the importance of approaching God with reverence and awe. To worship God in the beauty of holiness means to worship Him with pure hearts and minds, free from sin and impurity. It is a reminder that God is holy, and that we must approach Him with humility and respect.

In summary, Psalm 29:2 is a call to give glory to God and to worship Him in the beauty of holiness. It emphasizes God's greatness and power, and the importance of approaching Him with reverence and awe. It is a reminder that true worship is a matter of the heart, not just outward actions.

Prayer:

Dear God, As I come before You today, I am reminded of Your greatness and power. You are the Creator of the universe, the King of kings and Lord of lords, and the One who holds all power and authority. You are holy and righteous, and Your glory is beyond measure.

Lord, I want to give You all the glory and honor that You deserve. I want to worship You in the beauty of holiness, with pure hearts and minds, free from sin and impurity. Help me to approach You with reverence and awe, and to give You the worship and praise that You deserve.

As I worship You, I ask that You would fill me with Your Holy Spirit. Help me to worship You with my whole being, in spirit and in truth. May my worship be a reflection of my love for You, and a response to Your love and grace.

Lord, I pray that You would transform me by renewing my mind. Help me to think and act in a way that is consistent with Your will and Your Word. Give me the strength and courage to resist the temptations of this world, and to follow You wholeheartedly.

Thank You, God, for the privilege of worshiping You. May all that I do bring honor and glory to Your name, and may my life be a living sacrifice, holy and pleasing to You.

In Jesus' name I pray, Amen.

DAY FIVE

"God is Spirit, and those who worship Him must worship in spirit and truth." - John 4:24

John 4:24 is a powerful verse that speaks to the heart of true worship. In this passage, Jesus is speaking to a Samaritan woman at a well, and He tells her that God is Spirit, and those who worship Him must worship in spirit and truth.

The phrase "God is Spirit" emphasizes that God is not limited by physical form or location. He is present everywhere and at all times, and He is not bound by the constraints of this world. He is a spiritual being, and those who worship Him must approach Him in a spiritual way.

The phrase "worship in spirit and truth" emphasizes the importance of worshiping God with our whole being, in spirit and in truth. True worship is not just a matter of external actions or rituals, but a matter of the heart and our alignment with God's truth. It is a response to God's love and grace, and a reflection of our love for Him.

John 4:24 is a reminder that true worship is not just about external actions, but about the condition of our hearts. It is a call to worship God with all of our being, in spirit and in truth, and to seek His will in all that we do.
It reminds us that worship is not just a matter of outward actions or cultural tradition, but a matter of the heart and our alignment with God's truth.

Prayer:

Dear God, as I come before You today, I am reminded of Your call to true worship. You desire that I worship You in spirit and in truth, with all of my heart, soul, mind, and strength.

Lord, I ask that You would fill me with Your Holy Spirit, and help me to worship You with my whole being. May my worship be a reflection of my love for You, and a response to Your love and grace.

As I worship You, I ask that You would help me to align my heart and mind with Your truth. Guide me by Your Word and Your Spirit, and help me to worship You in a way that is pleasing to You.

Lord, I pray that You would deepen my relationship with You through worship. Help me to draw closer to You, to know You more intimately, and to experience Your presence in my life. May my worship be a catalyst for transformation, as You renew my mind and transform me into the image of Your Son.

Thank You, God, for the privilege of worshiping You. May all that I do bring honor and glory to Your name, and may my life be a living sacrifice, holy and pleasing to You.

In Jesus' name I pray, Amen.

DAY SIX

"Oh, magnify the Lord with me, and let us exalt His name together." -
Psalm 34:3

Psalm 34:3 is a powerful verse that emphasizes the importance of giving glory to God. The psalmist declares, "Oh, magnify the Lord with me, and let us exalt His name together." The word "magnify" means to make something appear larger or more important than it actually is. In this context, it means to give God the honor and recognition that He deserves.

The verse emphasizes that God is worthy of our worship and praise. He is the Creator of the universe, the King of kings and Lord of lords, and the One who holds all power and authority. He is holy and righteous, and His glory is beyond measure.

The phrase "let us exalt His name together" emphasizes the importance of corporate worship. We are called to worship God not only as individuals, but also as a community of believers. When we come together to worship, we encourage and strengthen one another, and we give glory to God in a powerful way.

Psalm 34:3 is a call to give glory to God and to exalt His name together. It emphasizes God's greatness and power, and the importance of corporate worship. It is a reminder that God is worthy of our worship and praise, and that true worship is a matter of the heart, not just outward actions.

Prayer:

Father, As I come before You today, I am reminded of Your greatness and power. You are the Creator of the universe, the King of kings and Lord of lords, and the One who holds all power and authority. You are holy and righteous, and Your glory is beyond measure.

Lord, I want to magnify Your name and give You the honor and recognition that You deserve. Help me to see You as larger than life, as more important than anything or anyone else. May my heart be filled with a sense of awe and reverence for You.

18

As I worship You, I ask that You would help me to exalt Your name together with other believers. Help me to be a part of a community of worshipers who encourage and strengthen one another, and who give glory to You in a powerful way.

Lord, I pray that You would transform me by renewing my mind. Help me to think and act in a way that is consistent with Your will and Your Word. Give me the strength and courage to resist the temptations of this world, and to follow You wholeheartedly.

Thank You, God, for the privilege of worshiping You. May all that I do bring honor and glory to Your name, and may my life be a living sacrifice, holy and pleasing to You.

In Jesus' name I pray, Amen.

DAY SEVEN

"Let them praise His name with the dance; let them sing praises to Him with the timbrel and harp." - Psalm 149:3

Psalm 149:3 is a part of a psalm that celebrates God's goodness and power. The verse reads, "Let them praise his name with dancing, making melody to him with tambourine and lyre!" This verse encourages people to praise God with joy and exuberance, using music and dance to express their gratitude and love for Him.

The context of this psalm is important to understand the meaning of this verse. The psalmist is calling on the people of God to praise Him for His faithfulness and salvation. The psalm begins by urging the people to sing a new song to the Lord and to rejoice in His goodness. The psalmist then goes on to describe how God takes pleasure in His people and how He defends them against their enemies.

In the midst of this celebration, Psalm 149:3 encourages the people to use music and dance as a way to express their joy and gratitude to God. The tambourine and lyre were common instruments used in worship during this time, and the psalmist is calling on the people to use these instruments to make a joyful noise to the Lord.

Psalm 149:3 is a call to worship and praise God with joy and exuberance. It reminds us that our worship should not be dull or lifeless, but should be filled with energy and excitement as we express our love and gratitude to our Creator.

Prayer:

Heavenly Father, As I come before You today, I am reminded of Your greatness and power. You are the Creator of the universe, the King of kings and Lord of lords, and the One who holds all power and authority. You are holy and righteous, and Your glory is beyond measure.

Lord, I want to praise Your name with dancing and make music to You with timbrel and harp. I want to express my joy and celebration in You through music and physical expression. Help me to worship You with my whole being.

As I worship You, I ask that You would fill me with Your Holy Spirit. Help me to worship You in spirit and in truth, with all of my heart, soul, mind, and strength. May my worship be a reflection of my love for You, and a response to Your love and grace.

Lord, I pray that You would use music to move my heart and mind, and to lift me up in worship. Help me to use music to honor You and to bring glory to Your name. May my worship inspire others to draw closer to You and to experience Your presence in their lives.

Thank You, God, for the privilege of worshiping You. May all that I do bring honor and glory to Your name, and may my life be a living sacrifice, holy and pleasing to You.

In Jesus' name I pray, Amen.

DAY EIGHT

"Sing to the Lord, all the earth; proclaim the good news of His salvation from day to day." - 1 Chronicles 16:23

In the context of worship, 1 Chronicles 16:23 emphasizes the importance of singing and proclaiming God's salvation. This verse encourages all people, regardless of their nationality or background, to join together in worshiping God. It emphasizes that worship is not just a personal, individual activity, but a communal one that involves the entire earth.

Furthermore, the verse highlights the importance of joy and thanksgiving in worship. Singing to the Lord is not just about reciting words, but about expressing genuine joy and gratitude for God's goodness and mercy. This is a common theme throughout the Bible, as many psalms and other passages speak about the importance of praising God with joy and thanksgiving.

1 Chronicles 16:23 is a powerful reminder of the importance of worship in the life of a believer. It encourages us to come together in community to sing and proclaim God's salvation, and to do so with joy and thanksgiving in our hearts.

Prayer:

Lord God Almighty,

I come before You today with a heart full of gratitude and thanksgiving. You are the Creator of the universe, the King of kings and Lord of lords, and the One who holds all power and authority. You are holy and righteous, and Your love and mercy are beyond measure.

Today, I want to sing to You and proclaim Your salvation day after day. I want to acknowledge Your goodness and grace in my life, and share the good news of Your salvation with others. Help me to remember Your faithfulness and to give thanks to You in all circumstances.

As I worship You, I ask that You would fill me with Your Holy Spirit. Help me to worship You in spirit and in truth, with all of my heart, soul, mind, and strength. May my worship be a reflection of my love for You, and a response to Your love and grace.

Lord, I pray that You would use me to share Your salvation with others. Help me to be a witness to Your love and grace, and to lead others to You. May my life be a shining example of Your goodness and mercy.

Thank You, God, for the privilege of worshiping You. May all that I do bring honor and glory to Your name, and may my life be a living sacrifice, holy and pleasing to You.

In Jesus' name I pray, Amen.

DAY NINE

"Give unto the Lord the glory due to His name; worship the Lord in the beauty of holiness." – Psalm 29:2

As we can see Psalm 29:2, is a call to recognize God's greatness and to give Him the honor and praise that He deserves. This recognition of God's greatness should lead us to worship Him with reverence and respect, recognizing that He is holy and deserving of our worship.

To truly give God the glory due to His name, we must first have a proper understanding of who He is. We must recognize that God is the Creator and Sustainer of all things, and that He is infinitely wise, powerful, and loving. This understanding of God's greatness should lead us to praise Him and give Him the honor that He deserves.

Furthermore, the call to "worship the Lord in the beauty of holiness" reminds us that our approach to God should be one of reverence and respect. This means that we should strive to live holy lives, avoiding sin and pursuing righteousness. As we seek to honor God in all that we do, we will find that our worship of Him becomes more genuine and heartfelt.

Ultimately, Psalm 29:2 is a call to live lives that are dedicated to honoring God and giving Him the glory that He deserves. As we recognize His greatness and approach Him with reverence and respect, we will find that our worship becomes more meaningful and our lives become more aligned with His will.

Prayer:

Lord Almighty, I come before You today with a heart full of reverence and awe. You are the Creator of the universe, the King of kings and Lord of lords, and the One who holds all power and authority. You are holy and righteous, and Your glory is beyond measure.

Today, I want to ascribe to You the glory due Your name. You deserve all the honor and recognition that I can give You. Help me to worship You in a way that reflects Your holiness and greatness. May my worship be a reflection of my love for You, and a response to Your love and grace.

As I worship You, I ask that You would fill me with Your Holy Spirit. Help me to worship You in spirit and in truth, with all of my heart, soul, mind, and strength. May my worship be pleasing to You, and may it bring glory to Your name.

Lord, I pray that You would help me to approach You with reverence and awe. Help me to see You as the holy and righteous God that You are, and to honor You with all that I am. May my life be a living sacrifice, holy and pleasing to You.

Thank You, God, for the privilege of worshiping You. May all that I do bring honor and glory to Your name, and may my life be a shining example of Your goodness and mercy.

In Jesus' name I pray, Amen.

DAY TEN

"For You alone are holy. For all nations shall come and worship before You, for Your judgments have been manifested." - Revelation 15:4

In the book of Revelation, chapter 15, John the Apostle has a vision of seven angels holding seven plagues, which are the last judgments of God upon the earth. In the midst of this vision, John sees a group of people standing beside a sea of glass, holding harps and singing a song of praise to God. The song begins with the words, "For You alone are holy."

This phrase is a declaration of the holiness of God, which is a central theme throughout the Bible. Holiness refers to God's absolute purity and perfection, which sets Him apart from all created beings. The fact that God is holy means that He is completely separate from sin and evil, and that He is worthy of our worship and adoration.

The song goes on to say that "all nations shall come and worship before You," which is a reference to the ultimate triumph of God's kingdom over all the nations of the earth. This is a vision of the future, when all people will acknowledge the sovereignty of God and worship Him alone.

The final phrase of the song, "for Your judgments have been manifested," refers to the fact that God's judgments have been made known to the world. The plagues that John sees in his vision are a manifestation of God's judgment upon the earth, and they serve as a warning to all people to repent and turn to God.

Overall, this passage emphasizes the holiness of God, the ultimate triumph of His kingdom, and the importance of repentance in the face of God's judgment. It is a powerful reminder that our ultimate allegiance should be to God alone, who is worthy of all our worship and praise.

Prayer:

Lord God, I come before You today with a heart full of reverence and awe. You are the Creator of the universe, the King of kings and Lord of lords, and the One who holds all power and authority. You alone are holy, and Your glory is beyond measure.

Today, I want to fear You and bring glory to Your name. You are worthy of all honor and recognition, and I want to worship You with all that I am. Help me to see You as the holy and righteous God that You are, and to honor You with my whole being.

As I worship You, I ask that You would fill me with Your Holy Spirit. Help me to worship You in spirit and in truth, with all of my heart, soul, mind, and strength. May my worship be pleasing to You, and may it bring glory to Your name.

Lord, I pray that You would help me to acknowledge Your greatness and holiness. Help me to see You as the one true God, and to worship You with reverence and awe. May my life be a reflection of Your goodness and mercy, and may others be drawn to You through my worship and witness.

Thank You, God, for the privilege of worshiping You. May all that I do bring honor and glory to Your name, and may my life be a living sacrifice, holy and pleasing to You.

In Jesus' name I pray, Amen.

DAY ELEVEN

"Praise the Lord! Oh, give thanks to the Lord, for He is good! For His mercy endures forever." - Psalm 106:1

Psalm 106:1 is a declaration of praise and thanksgiving to God, acknowledging His goodness and mercy. The psalmist begins by exclaiming "Praise the Lord!" This is a common phrase used throughout the book of Psalms to express adoration and worship towards God.

The psalmist then goes on to say "Oh, give thanks to the Lord, for He is good!" This is a call to action, urging the reader to express gratitude towards God for His goodness. The goodness of God is a recurring theme in the Bible, and is often associated with His love, compassion, and faithfulness towards His people.

The psalmist then declares that "His mercy endures forever." This is a powerful statement that emphasizes the unchanging nature of God's mercy. No matter what we may do or how far we may stray, God's mercy is always available to us. This is a comforting thought for those who may be struggling or feeling lost, as it reminds us that we are never beyond the reach of God's grace.

Overall, Psalm 106:1 is a beautiful expression of praise and thanksgiving to God. It reminds us of His goodness and mercy, and encourages us to give thanks for all that He has done for us. It is a powerful reminder of the love and faithfulness of God, and a source of comfort and hope for all who read it.

Prayer:

My Gracious Heavenly Father, I come before You today with a heart full of gratitude and thanksgiving. You are the Creator of the universe, the King of kings and Lord of lords, and the One who holds all power and authority. You are good and Your love endures forever.

Today, I want to praise You and give thanks to You. You have blessed me in countless ways, and I am grateful for Your faithfulness and love. Help me to remember Your goodness and to give thanks to You in all

28

circumstances.

As I worship You, I ask that You would fill me with Your Holy Spirit. Help me to worship You in spirit and in truth, with all of my heart, soul, mind, and strength. May my worship be a reflection of my love for You, and a response to Your love and grace.

Lord, I pray that You would help me to see Your blessings in my life. Help me to remember Your faithfulness and to give thanks to You for all that You have done. May my life be a testimony to Your goodness and mercy.

Thank You, God, for the privilege of worshiping You. May all that I do bring honor and glory to Your name, and may my life be a living sacrifice, holy and pleasing to You.

In Jesus' name I pray, Amen.

DAY TWELVE

"Let everything that has breath praise the Lord. Praise the Lord!" - Psalm 150:6

Psalm 150 is the final psalm in the book of Psalms, and it is a powerful and joyous call to praise God. The psalmist encourages all of creation to join in the praise of God, from the heavens above to the earth below. The psalmist declares that everything that has breath should praise the Lord, and that includes all living creatures.

The psalmist acknowledges that God is worthy of praise for all of His mighty acts and His surpassing greatness. God is the creator of all things, and He sustains the world with His power and love. The psalmist encourages all people to praise God for His goodness and His faithfulness, and to give thanks to Him for all that He has done.

The psalmist also calls upon all people to praise God with all of their might. This includes using musical instruments, singing, dancing, and shouting with joy. The psalmist recognizes that praising God is not just a matter of words, but it is an expression of the heart. When we praise God with all of our being, we are acknowledging His greatness and His love for us.

The final verse of Psalm 150 is a powerful declaration of praise: "Let everything that has breath praise the Lord. Praise the Lord!" This verse is a reminder that all of creation is called to praise God. It is a call to action for all people to join in the praise of God, and to give Him the honor and glory that He deserves. Let us join in the praise of God, and let everything that has breath praise the Lord! Praise the Lord!

Prayer:

Lord God Almighty, I come before You today with a heart full of praise and thanksgiving. You are the Creator of the universe, the King of kings and Lord of lords, and the One who holds all power and authority. You are

30

great and Your name is to be praised.

Today, I want to join with all living beings in giving You praise. You have blessed me in countless ways, and I am grateful for Your goodness and mercy. Help me to remember Your faithfulness and to continually acknowledge and praise You.

As I worship You, I ask that You would fill me with Your Holy Spirit. Help me to worship You in spirit and in truth, with all of my heart, soul, mind, and strength. May my worship be a reflection of my love for You, and a response to Your love and grace.

Lord, I pray that You would help me to continually give You praise. May my life be a testimony to Your greatness and power, and may others be drawn to You through my worship and witness.

Thank You, God, for the privilege of worshiping You. May all that I do bring honor and glory to Your name, and may my life be a living sacrifice, holy and pleasing to You.

In Jesus' name I pray,
Amen.

DAY THIRTEEN

"I will praise You, O Lord, with my whole heart; I will tell of all Your marvelous works." - Psalm 9:1

Psalm 9:1 is a powerful verse that calls us to give thanks to God with all our hearts. It is a reminder that God is the source of all blessings and that we should acknowledge His goodness in our lives. The verse also encourages us to share our testimonies of God's wonderful deeds with others, which can serve as a source of inspiration and encouragement.

Giving thanks to God is an act of worship that recognizes His sovereignty and goodness. When we give thanks to God, we acknowledge that He is the source of all blessings and that we owe everything to Him. It is a way to express our gratitude for His love and mercy, and to honor Him with our words and actions.

The phrase "with all my heart" emphasizes the importance of wholeheartedly giving thanks to God. It means that we should not hold back in expressing our gratitude and that we should give thanks to God with sincerity and authenticity. It is a call to give thanks to God not just with our lips but also with our hearts.

The phrase "I will tell of all Your wonderful deeds" highlights the importance of sharing our testimonies of God's goodness with others. Our testimonies can serve as a source of inspiration and encouragement to others who may be going through difficult times. It is a way to give glory to God and to testify to His faithfulness and love.

Psalm 9:1 is a call to give thanks to God with all our hearts and to share our testimonies of His wonderful deeds with others. It is a reminder that God is the source of all blessings and that we should acknowledge His goodness in our lives. Giving thanks to God is an act of worship that honors Him and expresses our gratitude for His love and mercy.

Prayer:

Lord God Almighty,

I come before You today with a heart full of gratitude and thanksgiving. You are the Creator of the universe, the King of kings and Lord of lords, and the One who holds all power and authority. I want to give thanks to You with all my heart and tell of all Your wonderful deeds.

Thank You, God, for all the blessings You have bestowed upon me. I am grateful for Your love and mercy, for Your provision and protection, and for Your faithfulness and grace. Help me to remember Your goodness and to give thanks to You in all circumstances.

As I worship You, I ask that You would fill me with Your Holy Spirit. Help me to worship You in spirit and in truth, with all of my heart, soul, mind, and strength. May my worship be a reflection of my love for You, and a response to Your love and grace.

Lord, I pray that You would help me to share my testimonies of Your wonderful deeds with others. May my life be a testimony to Your faithfulness and love, and may others be drawn to You through my worship and witness.

Thank You, God, for the privilege of worshiping You. May all that I do bring honor and glory to Your name, and may my life be a living sacrifice, holy and pleasing to You.

In Jesus' name I pray,
Amen.

DAY FOURTEEN

"Worship the Lord with gladness; come before Him with joyful songs."-
Psalm 100:2

Psalm 100 is a psalm of thanksgiving and praise, written to encourage God's people to worship Him with gladness and joy. The psalm begins with a call to shout for joy to the Lord, all the earth, and to serve the Lord with gladness. The psalmist then reminds the people that the Lord is God and that He made us, and we are His people, the sheep of His pasture.

The psalmist then goes on to encourage the people to enter His gates with thanksgiving and His courts with praise, giving thanks to Him and praising His name. The psalmist emphasizes the importance of worshiping the Lord with gladness and joy, recognizing that the Lord is good and His love endures forever.

The verse "Worship the Lord with gladness; come before Him with joyful songs" (Psalm 100:2) is a call to worship God with a joyful heart, recognizing that He is worthy of our praise and adoration. The psalmist is reminding us that worship is not just a duty or obligation, but it is an opportunity to express our love and gratitude to God for all that He has done for us.

The phrase "come before Him with joyful songs" emphasizes the importance of music in worship. Music has the power to touch our hearts and souls in a way that words alone cannot. It allows us to express our emotions and connect with God on a deeper level.

In conclusion, Psalm 100 is a powerful reminder of the importance of worshiping God with gladness and joy. It encourages us to enter into His presence with thanksgiving and praise, recognizing that He is good and His love endures forever. As we worship Him with joyful songs, we are reminded of His greatness and goodness, and we are filled with a sense of peace and joy that can only come from Him.

Prayer:

Lord God Almighty,

I come before You today with a heart full of joy and gladness. You are the Creator of the universe, the King of kings and Lord of lords, and the One who holds all power and authority. I want to worship You with gladness and come before You with joyful songs.

Thank You, God, for all the blessings You have bestowed upon me. I am grateful for Your love and mercy, for Your provision and protection, and for Your faithfulness and grace. Help me to remember Your goodness and to worship You with joy and enthusiasm.

As I worship You, I ask that You would fill me with Your Holy Spirit. Help me to worship You in spirit and in truth, with all of my heart, soul, mind, and strength. May my worship be a reflection of my love for You, and a response to Your love and grace.

Lord, I pray that You would help me to use music and song to worship You. May the melodies and lyrics of my songs be a pleasing offering to You, and may they express the joy and gladness that I feel in my heart.

Thank You, God, for the privilege of worshiping You. May all that I do bring honor and glory to Your name, and may my life be a living sacrifice, holy and pleasing to You.

In Jesus' name I pray,
Amen.

DAY FIFTEEN

"Exalt the Lord our God and worship at His footstool; He is holy." - Psalm 99:5

Psalm 99 is one of the many psalms in the Bible that is filled with praise and worship. In this particular verse, the psalmist is exhorting the people of God to exalt the Lord and worship at His footstool. The phrase "Exalt the Lord our God" is a call to lift up and magnify the name of God, acknowledging His greatness and sovereignty over all things.

The second part of the verse, "and worship at His footstool," is a reference to the temple in Jerusalem where God's presence was believed to dwell. The footstool represents the physical manifestation of God's presence on earth, and the act of worshiping at His footstool is a way of acknowledging His presence and giving Him the honor and glory that He deserves.

The final phrase, "He is holy," is a declaration of God's holiness. The word "holy" means set apart or separate, and is used to describe God's perfect and pure nature. It is a reminder that God is not like any other being in the universe, but is completely unique and deserving of our worship and adoration.

Overall, this verse is a call to worship and praise God for who He is and what He has done. It is a reminder that God is holy and deserving of our reverence and awe, and that we should approach Him with humility and gratitude. As we exalt the Lord and worship at His footstool, we are acknowledging His greatness and aligning ourselves with His will and purpose for our lives.

Prayer:

Heavenly Father, I come before You today with a heart full of reverence and awe. You are the Creator of the universe, the King of kings and Lord of lords, and the One who holds all power and authority. I want to exalt You and worship at Your footstool, for You are holy.

Thank You, God, for all the blessings You have bestowed upon me. I am grateful for Your love and mercy, for Your provision and protection, and for Your faithfulness and grace. Help me to remember Your greatness and holiness, and to approach You with humility and reverence.

As I worship You, I ask that You would fill me with Your Holy Spirit. Help me to worship You in spirit and in truth, with all of my heart, soul, mind, and strength. May my worship be a reflection of my love for You, and a response to Your greatness and holiness.

Lord, I pray that You would help me to exalt You in all areas of my life. May I give You the highest place of honor in my thoughts, words, and actions. Help me to recognize Your sovereignty over all things and to acknowledge Your greatness in all circumstances.

Thank You, God, for the privilege of worshiping You. May all that I do bring honor and glory to Your name, and may my life be a living sacrifice, holy and pleasing to You.

In Jesus' name I pray,
Amen.

DAY SIXTEEN

"Come, let us bow down in worship, let us kneel before the Lord our Maker." -Psalm 95:6

Psalm 95 is a beautiful and powerful psalm that calls on all people to worship and praise the Lord. The psalm begins with a joyful invitation to come and sing praises to God, acknowledging Him as our rock and salvation. The psalmist then goes on to exhort the people to bow down in worship and kneel before the Lord our Maker, recognizing His sovereignty and majesty.

The phrase "Come, let us bow down in worship, let us kneel before the Lord our Maker" is a call to action, a call to recognize and honor God as the one who created us and sustains us. It is an invitation to enter into His presence with reverence and humility, acknowledging His greatness and goodness.

The psalmist goes on to remind us that God is the great King above all gods, the one who holds the depths of the earth and the heights of the mountains in His hands. He is the one who made the sea and the dry land, and the one who watches over us and cares for us.

The psalm then takes a sobering turn, warning us not to harden our hearts against God's voice, as the Israelites did in the wilderness. The psalmist reminds us that those who rebelled against God in the wilderness were not able to enter into His rest, and that we too must be careful not to turn away from God's voice and His call to worship and obedience.

Ultimately, Psalm 95 is a powerful reminder of the importance of worship and reverence in our relationship with God. It calls us to recognize God as our Maker and King, and to enter into His presence with humility and awe. It reminds us of the danger of hardening our hearts against God's voice, and the importance of remaining faithful and obedient to His call. As we bow down in worship and kneel before the Lord our Maker, may our hearts be filled with gratitude and praise for all that He has done for us.

Prayer:

Lord God, As I come before You today, I am filled with a heart of humility and reverence. You are the Creator of the universe, the King of kings and Lord of lords, and the One who holds all power and authority. I want to bow down in worship and kneel before You, my Maker.

Thank You, God, for all the blessings You have bestowed upon me. I am grateful for Your love and mercy, for Your provision and protection, and for Your faithfulness and grace. Help me to remember Your greatness and holiness, and to approach You with humility and reverence.

As I worship You, I ask that You would fill me with Your Holy Spirit. Help me to worship You in spirit and in truth, with all of my heart, soul, mind, and strength. May my worship be a reflection of my love for You, and a response to Your greatness and holiness.

Lord, I pray that You would help me to approach You with a heart of humility and reverence. May I recognize my position before You and acknowledge Your greatness and holiness. Help me to remember that I am in the presence of the holy and almighty God.

Thank You, God, for the privilege of worshiping You. May all that I do bring honor and glory to Your name, and may my life be a living sacrifice, holy and pleasing to You.

In Jesus' name I pray,
Amen.

DAY SEVENTEEN

"Sing to Him a new song; play skillfully, and shout for joy." -Psalm 33:3

Psalm 33:3 is a call to worship and praise God through singing and playing music. This verse is a reminder to believers that worship is not just about going through the motions, but about truly engaging with God and expressing our love and adoration for Him.

The phrase "Sing to Him a new song" is a common theme throughout the Psalms. It is a call to creativity and innovation in worship, encouraging us to come up with new ways to express our love for God. The word "new" suggests that worship should not become stale or repetitive, but should always be fresh and exciting.

The second part of the verse, "play skillfully," emphasizes the importance of excellence in worship. It is not enough to simply go through the motions; we must strive to do our best and offer our talents and abilities to God. Whether we are singing, playing an instrument, or leading worship in some other way, we should do so with skill and dedication.

Finally, the verse ends with a call to "shout for joy." This is a reminder that worship should be a joyful experience. We should not approach it with a sense of obligation or duty, but with a sense of excitement and enthusiasm. When we truly engage with God in worship, we cannot help but be filled with joy and gratitude.

In summary, Psalm 33:3 is a call to worship and praise God through singing, playing music, and shouting for joy. It reminds us to be creative, excellent, and joyful in our worship, always seeking new ways to express our love and adoration for God.

Prayer:

Lord God Almighty, As I come before You today, I am filled with a heart of worship and adoration. You are the Creator of the universe, the King of kings and Lord of lords, and the One who holds all power and authority. I want to sing to You a new song, to play skillfully, and to shout for joy.

Thank You, God, for all the blessings You have bestowed upon me. I am grateful for Your love and mercy, for Your provision and protection, and for Your faithfulness and grace. Help me to remember Your greatness and to worship You with all of my heart, soul, mind, and strength.

As I worship You, I ask that You would fill me with Your Holy Spirit. Help me to worship You in spirit and in truth, with all of my heart, soul, mind, and strength. May my worship be a reflection of my love for You, and a response to Your greatness and power.

Lord, I pray that You would help me to use my talents and abilities to honor You. May I offer my best to You in my worship, using my skills to bring glory to Your name. Help me to be creative and innovative in my worship, and to sing to You a new song.

Thank You, God, for the privilege of worshiping You. May all that I do bring honor and glory to Your name, and may my life be a living sacrifice, holy and pleasing to You.

In Jesus' name I pray,
Amen.

DAY EIGHTEEN

"And whatever you do in word or deed, do all in the name of the Lord Jesus, giving thanks to God the Father through Him." - Colossians 3:17

Colossians 3:17 is part of a larger passage in the New Testament where the apostle Paul is instructing the Colossians on how to live a life that is centered on Jesus Christ. Paul emphasizes that Christians are called to live a new life in Christ, and that this new life should be marked by a transformation in their thoughts, words, and actions.

In Colossians 3:17, Paul is reminding the Colossians that everything they do, whether in word or deed, should be done in the name of the Lord Jesus. This means that their actions and words should reflect the character of Christ and honor Him in all that they do. Paul is calling the Colossians to live a life that is centered on Jesus Christ, and to make Him the center of their thoughts, words, and actions.

The phrase "giving thanks to God the Father through him" is a reminder that Christians should be marked by gratitude and thankfulness. Paul is calling the Colossians to recognize God's blessings and to give thanks to Him for all that He has done for them. This is a reminder that the Christian life should be marked by a spirit of gratitude, recognizing that all blessings come from God.

Overall, Colossians 3:17 is a call to live a life that is centered on Jesus Christ and honors God in all aspects. It is a reminder that the Christian life is a new life, marked by a transformation in thoughts, words, and actions. It is also a reminder to be grateful and give thanks to God for all blessings.

Prayer:

Father, As I come before You today, I am filled with a heart of gratitude and thankfulness. You are the center of my life, and I want to honor You in all that I do, whether in word or deed. I pray that You would help me to reflect the character of Christ in my thoughts, words, and actions.

Thank You, God, for all the blessings You have bestowed upon me. I am grateful for Your love and mercy, for Your provision and protection, and for Your faithfulness and grace. Help me to remember that all blessings come from You, and to give thanks to You for all that You have done for me.

As I go about my day, I pray that You would guide me and direct me. Help me to make decisions that honor You and reflect Your character. May my words and actions be a reflection of Your love and grace, and may they bring glory to Your name.

Lord, I pray that You would help me to live a life that is centered on Jesus Christ. May He be the center of my thoughts, words, and actions, and may I honor Him in all that I do. Help me to be transformed by Your Spirit, and to live a life that is pleasing to You.

Thank You, God, for the privilege of knowing You and serving You. May all that I do bring honor and glory to Your name, and may my life be a living sacrifice, holy and pleasing to You.

In Jesus' name I pray,
Amen.

DAY NINETEEN

"Give thanks to the Lord and proclaim his greatness. Let the whole world know what he has done." - Psalm 105:1

Psalm 105:1 is an awesome reminder of the importance of giving thanks to God and proclaiming His greatness. The verse encourages us to share with the whole world what God has done in our lives. This is a call to action for every believer, reminding us to always be grateful for the blessings we receive from God and to share our testimony with others.

The context of Psalm 105 is a celebration of God's faithfulness to Israel. The psalmist recounts the history of Israel, from the time of Abraham to the Exodus and the entry into the Promised Land. Throughout this history, God remained faithful to His people, guiding them, protecting them, and providing for them.

The psalmist encourages the people of Israel to remember God's faithfulness and to give thanks for all that He has done. This is a reminder that even in difficult times, God is always with us, and we can trust in His love and provision.

As Christians, we can apply this message to our own lives. We should always be grateful for the blessings we receive from God, both big and small. We should also be willing to share our testimony with others, so that they too can see the goodness of God in our lives.

In addition to giving thanks, Psalm 105:1 also encourages us to proclaim God's greatness to the whole world. This means sharing the Gospel with others, so that they too can come to know God and experience His love and grace.

In conclusion, Psalm 105:1 is a powerful reminder of the importance of giving thanks to God and proclaiming His greatness. It encourages us to remember God's faithfulness in our own lives, and to share our testimony with others. As we do so, we can help to spread the Gospel and bring others into a closer relationship with God.

Prayer:

Lord God Almighty,

As I come before You today, I am filled with a heart of gratitude and thankfulness. You are the Creator of the universe, the King of kings and Lord of lords, and the One who holds all power and authority. I want to give thanks to You and proclaim Your greatness to the whole world.

Thank You, God, for all the blessings You have bestowed upon me. I am grateful for Your love and mercy, for Your provision and protection, and for Your faithfulness and grace. Help me to remember Your goodness and to give thanks to You for all that You have done for me.

As I go about my day, I pray that You would help me to proclaim Your greatness to the whole world. May I be a witness to Your love and grace, and may I share Your goodness with those around me. Help me to be a light in the darkness, and to bring hope and joy to those who need it.

Lord, I pray that You would help me to live a life that is pleasing to You. May my thoughts, words, and actions reflect Your character, and may I honor You in all that I do. Help me to be transformed by Your Spirit, and to live a life that brings glory to Your name.

In Jesus' name I pray,
Amen.

DAY TWENTY

"Ascribe to the Lord the glory due his name; worship the Lord in the splendor of his holiness." -Psalm 29:2

Psalm 29:2 is a powerful verse that emphasizes the importance of worshiping God with reverence and awe. The verse highlights the power of worship to connect us with God and to express our love and reverence for Him.

The verse emphasizes that God is deserving of our worship and adoration. He is the Creator of the universe, the King of kings and Lord of lords, and the One who holds all power and authority. He is great and His name is to be glorified.

The phrase "ascribe to the Lord the glory due his name" emphasizes the importance of giving God the honor and glory that He deserves. It is a call to recognize God's greatness and to acknowledge His holiness and power. It is a reminder that our worship should be characterized by reverence and awe.

The phrase "worship the Lord in the splendor of his holiness" emphasizes the importance of approaching God with humility and respect. It is a call to recognize God's holiness and to respond with worship and adoration. It is a reminder that our worship should be marked by reverence and awe, and that we should approach God with humility and respect.

In summary, Psalm 29:2 is a call to worship God with reverence and awe. It emphasizes God's greatness and power, and the importance of recognizing His holiness and giving Him the honor and glory that He deserves. It is a reminder that our worship should be characterized by humility and respect, and that we should approach God with reverence and awe.

Prayer:

Lord God Almighty, As I come before You today, I am filled with a heart of worship and adoration. You are the Creator of the universe, the King of kings and Lord of lords, and the One who holds all power and authority. I want to ascribe to You the glory due Your name and worship You in the splendor of Your holiness.

Thank You, God, for all the blessings You have bestowed upon me. I am grateful for Your love and mercy, for Your provision and protection, and for Your faithfulness and grace. Help me to remember Your greatness and to worship You with all of my heart, soul, mind, and strength.

As I worship You, I ask that You would fill me with Your Holy Spirit. Help me to worship You in spirit and in truth, with all of my heart, soul, mind, and strength. May my worship be a reflection of my love for You, and a response to Your greatness and power.

Lord, I pray that You would help me to approach You with reverence and awe. May I recognize Your holiness and respond with humility and respect. Help me to remember that You are the King of kings and Lord of lords, and that You are deserving of all honor and glory.

Thank You, God, for the privilege of worshiping You. May all that I do bring honor and glory to Your name, and may my life be a living sacrifice, holy and pleasing to You.

In Jesus' name I pray,
Amen.

DAY TWENTY-ONE

"Let the words of my mouth and the meditation of my heart be acceptable in Your sight, O Lord, my strength and my Redeemer." - Psalm 19:14

Psalm 19:14 is a wonderful verse that emphasizes the importance of the words we speak and the thoughts we think. The verse highlights the power of our words and thoughts to impact our relationship with God.

The verse emphasizes that our words and thoughts are important to God. They are a reflection of our heart and our relationship with Him. The psalmist is asking God to help him to speak and think in a way that is pleasing to Him.

The phrase "acceptable in your sight" emphasizes the importance of living a life that is pleasing to God. It is a call to recognize God's sovereignty and to seek to honor Him in all that we say and do. The psalmist is asking God to help him to live a life that is pleasing to Him.

The phrase "Oh Lord, my strength and my Redeemer" emphasizes the psalmist's relationship with God. He recognizes God as his Rock and his Redeemer, and he is seeking to honor Him in all that he says and does. It is a reminder that our relationship with God is central to our lives, and that we should seek to honor Him in all that we do.

Psalm 19:14 is a call to live a life that is pleasing to God. It emphasizes the importance of our words and thoughts, and the impact that they have on our relationship with Him. It is a reminder of the importance of honoring God in all that we say and do, and the role that our relationship with Him plays in our lives.

Prayer:

My heavenly Father, As I come before You today, I am reminded of the importance of my words and thoughts. I want to honor You in all that I say and do, and I ask that You would help me to speak and think in a way that

48

is pleasing to You.

May the words of my mouth and the meditation of my heart be pleasing in Your sight, O Lord, my Rock and my Redeemer. Help me to recognize Your sovereignty and to seek to honor You in all that I say and do. May my words and thoughts be a reflection of my love for You and my desire to serve You.

Lord, I pray that You would help me to live a life that is pleasing to You. May my words and thoughts be a reflection of Your love and grace, and may they bring honor and glory to Your name. Help me to remember that my relationship with You is central to my life, and that I should seek to honor You in all that I do.

Thank You, God, for the privilege of knowing You and serving You. May all that I do bring honor and glory to Your name, and may my life be a living sacrifice, holy and pleasing to You.

In Jesus' name I pray,
Amen.

DAY TWENTY-TWO

"Enter into His gates with thanksgiving, and into His courts with praise. Be thankful to Him, and bless His name." - Psalm 100:4

Psalm 100 is a beautiful hymn of praise and thanksgiving to God. The psalmist begins by calling all the earth to make a joyful noise to the Lord and to serve Him with gladness. The psalmist then reminds us that God is our Creator and we are His people. We are called to enter into His gates with thanksgiving and into His courts with praise. This is an invitation to come before God with a heart full of gratitude and reverence.

The psalmist goes on to say that we should be thankful to God and bless His name. This is a call to worship and praise God for who He is and for all the blessings He has bestowed upon us. We are to remember that every good and perfect gift comes from God, and we should give Him the honor and praise He deserves.

The phrase "Enter into His gates with thanksgiving, and into His courts with praise" is a reminder that we are coming before a holy God and should approach Him with reverence and gratitude. The gates and courts of the temple were places of worship and sacrifice, and we are called to enter into these places with a heart of thanksgiving and praise.

The psalmist continues by saying that God is good and His mercy endures forever. This is a reminder that God is always faithful, even when we are not. His love and mercy are never-ending, and we can trust in Him to always be there for us.

In conclusion, Psalm 100 is a beautiful reminder of the importance of worship and praise in our lives. We are called to come before God with a heart of gratitude and reverence, acknowledging Him as our Creator and the source of all our blessings. We should be thankful to Him and bless His name, recognizing His goodness and mercy towards us. As we enter into His gates with thanksgiving and into His courts with praise, may we be reminded of the great love and faithfulness of our God.

Prayer:

Lord God Almighty, As I come before You today, I am filled with a heart of gratitude and thanksgiving. You are the Creator of the universe, the King of kings and Lord of lords, and the One who holds all power and authority. I want to enter Your gates with thanksgiving and Your courts with praise, and give thanks to You and praise Your name.

Thank You, God, for all the blessings You have bestowed upon me. I am grateful for Your love and mercy, for Your provision and protection, and for Your faithfulness and grace. Help me to remember Your goodness and to give thanks to You for all that You have done for me.

As I worship You, I ask that You would fill me with Your Holy Spirit. Help me to worship You in spirit and in truth, with all of my heart, soul, mind, and strength. May my worship be a reflection of my love for You, and a response to Your greatness and power.

Lord, I pray that You would help me to live a life that is pleasing to You. May my words and thoughts be pleasing in Your sight, and may I honor You in all that I do. Help me to recognize Your blessings and to give thanks to You for all that You have done for me.

Thank You, God, for the privilege of worshiping You. May all that I do bring honor and glory to Your name, and may my life be a living sacrifice, holy and pleasing to You.

In the Name of Jesus,
Amen.

DAY TWENTY-THREE

"Bless the Lord, O my soul; and all that is within me, bless His holy name!" - Psalm 103:1

Psalm 103 is a beautiful hymn of praise and thanksgiving to God. It begins with an exhortation to the soul to bless the Lord with all that is within it. The psalmist calls upon his soul to remember all the benefits that God has bestowed upon him and to bless His holy name.

The psalmist acknowledges that God forgives all his sins and heals all his diseases. He redeems his life from the pit and crowns him with love and compassion. The psalmist is overwhelmed by God's goodness and mercy, and he praises God for His steadfast love and faithfulness.

The psalmist goes on to describe how God's love and mercy extend to all who fear Him. God is slow to anger and abounding in love, and He does not treat us as our sins deserve. Instead, He has removed our sins from us as far as the east is from the west.

The psalmist then reflects on the brevity of human life and the greatness of God's love. He compares our lives to grass that withers and flowers that fade, but God's love endures forever. The psalmist is awed by the majesty of God's creation and the wonder of His works.

The psalm concludes with a call to all of creation to bless the Lord. The psalmist exhorts the angels, the heavenly hosts, and all of God's creation to praise and worship Him. He ends with a final exhortation to his own soul to bless the Lord and to never forget all of His benefits.

In summary, Psalm 103 is a beautiful hymn of praise and thanksgiving to God. It reminds us of the greatness of God's love and mercy and calls us to bless His holy name with all that is within us. It is a powerful reminder that God is worthy of our praise and worship, and that we should never forget all the benefits that He has bestowed upon us.

Prayer:

Lord God Almighty, As I come before You today, I am filled with a heart of praise and adoration. You are the Creator of the universe, the King of kings and Lord of lords, and the One who holds all power and authority. I want to praise You with my whole being, and give You the honor and glory that You deserve.

Praise the Lord, my soul; all my inmost being, praise Your holy name. Help me to recognize Your greatness and to respond with worship and adoration. May my worship be characterized by my whole being, and may I approach You with all that I am.

Thank You, God, for all the blessings You have bestowed upon me. I am grateful for Your love and mercy, for Your provision and protection, and for Your faithfulness and grace. Help me to remember Your goodness and to give You the honor and glory that You deserve.

As I worship You, I ask that You would fill me with Your Holy Spirit. Help me to worship You in spirit and in truth, with all of my heart, soul, mind, and strength. May my worship be a reflection of my love for You, and a response to Your greatness and power.

Thank You, God, for the privilege of worshiping You. May all that I do bring honor and glory to Your name, and may my life be a living sacrifice, holy and pleasing to You.

In Jesus' name I pray,
Amen.

DAY TWENTY-FOUR

"For great is the Lord and greatly to be praised; He is to be feared above all gods." - 1 Chronicles 16:25

This verse is a part of a longer passage that is attributed to King David, who is believed to have written it as a song of thanksgiving and praise after the Ark of the Covenant was brought to Jerusalem.

The passage begins by exhorting the people of Israel to give thanks to the Lord and to call upon His name. It then goes on to recount the wonders that God has done for His people, from the time of Abraham and Isaac to the time of Moses and the Exodus from Egypt. The passage also includes a prayer of blessing for the people of Israel, asking God to remember His covenant with them and to bless them with peace and prosperity.

The verse in question, "For great is the Lord and greatly to be praised; He is to be feared above all gods," is a declaration of the greatness of God. The use of the word "Lord" with a capital "L" is a reference to the God of Israel, who is considered to be the one true God. The verse emphasizes the importance of praising and worshipping God, and acknowledges His supremacy over all other gods.

The phrase "He is to be feared above all gods" is a reminder that the God of Israel is not to be taken lightly. The word "feared" here does not mean fear in the sense of being scared, but rather in the sense of having reverence and respect for God's power and authority. This is a common theme throughout the Bible, where God is often described as being a just and righteous judge who demands obedience and respect from His people.

The verse "For great is the Lord and greatly to be praised; He is to be feared above all gods" is a powerful declaration of the greatness of God and the importance of praising and worshipping Him. It is a reminder that God is not to be taken lightly, but rather deserves our utmost respect and reverence.

Prayer:

54

God, as I come before You today, I am reminded of Your greatness and power. You are the Creator of the universe, the King of kings and Lord of lords, and the One who holds all power and authority. I recognize that You are most worthy of praise, and that there is no other God like You.

For great is the Lord and most worthy of praise; You are to be feared above all gods. Help me to approach You with reverence and awe, recognizing Your sovereignty and power. May I always remember that You are unique and supreme, and that You are deserving of all honor and glory.

Thank You, God, for all the blessings You have bestowed upon me. I am grateful for Your love and mercy, for Your provision and protection, and for Your faithfulness and grace. Help me to remember Your greatness and power, and to give You the honor and praise that You deserve.

As I worship You, I ask that You would fill me with Your Holy Spirit. Help me to worship You in spirit and in truth, with all of my heart, soul, mind, and strength. May my worship be a reflection of my love for You, and a response to Your greatness and power.

Thank You, God, for the privilege of knowing You and serving You. May all that I do bring honor and glory to Your name, and may my life be a living sacrifice, holy and pleasing to You.

In the Name of Jesus,
Amen.

DAY TWENTY-FIVE

"I will praise the name of God with a song, and will magnify Him with thanksgiving." - Psalm 69:30

Psalm 69:30 is a powerful verse that emphasizes the importance of praising God with a thankful heart. The verse highlights the power of gratitude and praise in our relationship with God.

The verse emphasizes that God is deserving of our praise and adoration.

The phrase "I will praise God's name in song" emphasizes the importance of expressing our love and adoration for God. It is a call to acknowledge God's greatness and to respond with worship and adoration. It is a reminder that our worship should be marked by gratitude and praise, and that we should approach God with a spirit of thanksgiving and praise.

The phrase "glorify him with thanksgiving" emphasizes the importance of recognizing God's blessings and giving Him thanks for all that He has done for us. It is a reminder that our worship should be characterized by a spirit of gratitude and thankfulness, and that we should approach God with a heart of thanksgiving.

In summary, Psalm 69:30 is a call to praise God with a thankful heart. It emphasizes God's greatness and power, and the importance of recognizing His blessings and giving Him the honor and glory that He deserves. It is a reminder that our worship should be characterized by a spirit of gratitude and thankfulness, and that we should approach God with a heart of thanksgiving.

Prayer:

Heavenly Father, As I come before You today, I am filled with a heart of gratitude and thanksgiving. You are the Creator of the universe, the King of kings and Lord of lords, and the One who holds all power and authority. I want to praise Your name in song and glorify You with thanksgiving.

Thank You, God, for all the blessings You have bestowed upon me. I am grateful for Your love and mercy, for Your provision and protection, and for Your faithfulness and grace. Help me to remember Your goodness and to give You thanks for all that You have done for me.

As I worship You, I ask that You would fill me with Your Holy Spirit. Help me to worship You in spirit and in truth, with all of my heart, soul, mind, and strength. May my worship be a reflection of my love for You, and a response to Your greatness and power.

Lord, I pray that You would help me to live a life that is pleasing to You. May my words and thoughts be pleasing in Your sight, and may I honor You in all that I do. Help me to recognize Your blessings and to give You thanks for all that You have done for me.

Thank You, God, for the privilege of worshiping You. May all that I do bring honor and glory to Your name, and may my life be a living sacrifice, holy and pleasing to You.

In Jesus' name I pray,
Amen.

DAY TWENTY-SIX

"Let us shout joyfully to the Rock of our salvation. Let us come before His presence with thanksgiving; let us shout joyfully to Him with psalms." - Psalm 95:1-2

Psalm 95:1-2 is a call to worship and praise God, the Rock of our salvation. The psalmist encourages us to shout joyfully to God, to come before His presence with thanksgiving, and to sing psalms of praise to Him. This passage emphasizes the importance of expressing our gratitude and reverence to God through worship.

The phrase "Rock of our salvation" refers to God as the foundation and source of our salvation. The psalmist acknowledges that salvation comes from God alone, and therefore, we should give Him praise and thanksgiving for His mercy and grace.

The call to shout joyfully and sing psalms is an invitation to express our emotions and feelings towards God. This is not a passive act of worship, but an active and enthusiastic response to God's goodness and faithfulness. By shouting and singing, we declare our love and devotion to God and express our joy and gratitude for all that He has done for us.

In conclusion, Psalm 95:1-2 is a powerful reminder of the importance of worship and praise in our relationship with God. It encourages us to come before God with thanksgiving and joy, recognizing Him as the Rock of our salvation. As we worship and praise God, we are reminded of His goodness and faithfulness, and we are strengthened in our faith and trust in Him.

Prayer:

Lord God, As I come before You today, I am filled with a heart of joy and thanksgiving. You are the Creator of the universe, the King of kings and Lord of lords, and the One who holds all power and authority. I want to sing for joy to You and shout aloud to the Rock of my salvation.

Thank You, God, for all the blessings You have bestowed upon me. I am grateful for Your love and mercy, for Your provision and protection, and for Your faithfulness and grace. Help me to remember Your goodness and to give You thanks for all that You have done for me.

As I worship You, I ask that You would fill me with Your Holy Spirit. Help me to worship You in spirit and in truth, with all of my heart, soul, mind, and strength. May my worship be characterized by joy and celebration, and may I approach You with a heart of thanksgiving.

Lord, I pray that You would help me to live a life that is pleasing to You. May my words and thoughts be pleasing in Your sight, and may I honor You in all that I do. Help me to recognize Your blessings and to give You thanks for all that You have done for me.

Thank You, God, for the privilege of worshiping You. May all that I do bring honor and glory to Your name, and may my life be a living sacrifice, holy and pleasing to You.

In Jesus' name I pray,
Amen.

DAY TWENTY-SEVEN

"But you are a chosen generation, a royal priesthood, a holy nation, His own special people, that you may proclaim the praises of Him who called you out of darkness into His marvelous light." -1 Peter 2:9

In 1 Peter 2:9, the apostle Peter is addressing the believers in the early Christian church, reminding them of their identity as followers of Jesus Christ. He tells them that they are a chosen generation, a royal priesthood, a holy nation, and God's own special people.

Peter's words are significant because they remind the believers of their spiritual heritage and their role in the world. By calling them a "chosen generation," Peter is emphasizing that they have been specifically chosen by God to be part of his family. This is a reminder that their faith is not just a matter of personal preference, but it is part of a larger plan that God has for the world.

The phrase "royal priesthood" is also significant because it speaks to the believers' role as representatives of God to the world. In the Old Testament, the priesthood was a special group of people who were set apart to serve God in the temple. But now, Peter is saying that all believers are part of a new priesthood, one that serves God in the world by proclaiming his truth and living out his love.

The phrase "holy nation" speaks to the believers' identity as a community of faith. They are not just individuals who happen to believe in God, but they are part of a larger group of people who are committed to living out their faith together. This community is set apart from the world because of their commitment to God's ways and their willingness to love and serve others.

Finally, Peter calls the believers "God's own special people." This phrase emphasizes the believers' intimate relationship with God. They are not just servants or followers of God, but they are his children, loved and cherished by him.

Overall, Peter's words in 1 Peter 2:9 remind believers of their identity and their purpose in the world. They are part of a chosen generation, a royal priesthood, a holy nation, and God's own special people. Their role is to proclaim the praises of God and to live out their faith in a way that brings glory to him.

Prayer:

Lord God Almighty, As I come before You today, I am reminded of my identity and purpose in Christ. I am a chosen people, a royal priesthood, a holy nation, and Your special possession. Help me to live up to this calling and to serve You with all my heart, soul, mind, and strength.

Thank You, God, for calling me out of darkness into Your wonderful light. I am grateful for Your love and mercy, for Your grace and forgiveness, and for Your faithfulness and goodness. Help me to declare Your praises and to share the good news of salvation with others.

As I worship You, I ask that You would fill me with Your Holy Spirit. Help me to be a light in the darkness, pointing others to Your love and grace. May my life be a reflection of Your goodness and may my words and actions bring honor and glory to Your name.

Lord, I pray that You would help me to live a life that is pleasing to You. May I honor You in all that I do, and may my life be a living sacrifice, holy and pleasing to You. Help me to recognize my identity and purpose in Christ, and to live up to this calling with courage, faith, and love.

Thank You, God, for the privilege of serving You. May all that I do bring honor and glory to Your name, and may I be a vessel of Your love and grace to others.

In Jesus' name I pray,
Amen.

DAY TWENTY-EIGHT

"Oh, sing to the Lord a new song! Sing to the Lord, all the earth." - Psalm 96:1

Psalm 96:1 is a call to worship and praise God. The psalmist encourages all the earth to sing a new song to the Lord. This new song is a fresh expression of praise and adoration for God, and it is meant to be sung by all people, regardless of their background or nationality.

The idea of singing a new song to the Lord is a common theme throughout the Psalms. It is a way of expressing the joy and wonder of encountering God in a new and fresh way. The psalmist is inviting all of creation to join in this celebration of God's goodness and faithfulness.

The phrase "all the earth" in this verse is significant because it highlights the universal nature of God's love and grace. God's salvation is not limited to a particular group or nation, but is available to all who call upon the name of the Lord. The psalmist is inviting all people to join in this celebration of God's salvation and to lift their voices in praise and worship.

In addition to the call to sing a new song, Psalm 96 also emphasizes the greatness of God and the power of His salvation. The psalmist declares that God is worthy of all praise and honor, and that all other gods are mere idols. He also reminds us that God is the creator of all things and that He will one day judge the world in righteousness.

Psalm 96:1 is a powerful call to worship and praise God. It reminds us of the universal nature of God's love and salvation, and invites us to join in a celebration of His goodness and faithfulness. Whether we are singing a new song or simply lifting our voices in praise, let us always remember to give thanks to the Lord for all that He has done for us.

Prayer:

Lord God Almighty, I come before You today with a heart full of gratitude and thanksgiving. I am grateful for the gift of life, for the breath in my lungs, and for the opportunity to worship You. I thank You for Your goodness and faithfulness, and for the salvation that is available to all who call upon Your name.

Lord, please help me to sing a new song to You. I pray that You would give me fresh expressions of praise and adoration, and that I would never grow weary of lifting my voice in worship. Please help me to see Your greatness and power, and to declare Your goodness to all the earth.

I pray for all those who have not yet heard the good news of Your salvation. I ask that You would open their hearts and minds to receive Your love and grace, and that they would join me in singing a new song to You.

Lord, I know that You are the creator of all things, and that You will one day judge the world in righteousness. I pray that I would always be ready to meet You, and that I would live my life in a way that brings honor and glory to Your name.

In Jesus' name, I pray. Amen.

DAY TWENTY-NINE

"Give thanks to the Lord, for He is good; His love endures forever." - 1
Chronicles 16:34

This verse is a powerful statement from the Bible that emphasizes the
importance of gratitude and appreciation towards God. It is a part of a
larger passage that describes King David's celebration of the Ark of the
Covenant's arrival in Jerusalem.

In this passage, King David is filled with joy and gratitude towards God for
the return of the Ark, which symbolized God's presence among the
Israelites. He leads the people in a song of praise and thanksgiving, which
includes the verse, "Give thanks to the Lord, for He is good; His love
endures forever."

This verse reminds us that God is good and loving, and that we should be
grateful for all that He has done for us. It also emphasizes the importance
of recognizing God's enduring love, which is a constant presence in our
lives, even when we may not feel it.

As Christians, we are called to give thanks to God for all of His blessings
and to acknowledge His goodness and love towards us. This verse serves as
a reminder to cultivate an attitude of gratitude and to always give thanks to
God, no matter what our circumstances may be.

"Give thanks to the Lord, for He is good; His love endures forever" is a
powerful statement that reminds us of God's goodness and love towards us.
It is a call to cultivate an attitude of gratitude and to always give thanks to
God for all of His blessings.

Prayer:

*Dear God, I come before you today with a heart full of gratitude and
praise. I declare with confidence that I will bless You at all times, and Your
praise shall continually be in my mouth. I thank You for Your unending
love, grace, and mercy that sustain me through every season of life.*

Lord, I acknowledge that You are sovereign and in control of all things. I trust in Your protection and provision, even in the midst of difficult circumstances. I pray that Your name would be exalted and glorified in my life, and that Your praise would continually be on my lips.

Help me to have a heart of gratitude and thanksgiving, even in the midst of trials and hardships. May Your love and faithfulness be a constant source of strength and comfort to me.

In the name of Jesus, Amen.

DAY THIRTY

"I will bless the Lord at all times; His praise shall continually be in my mouth." - Psalm 34:1

Psalm 34:1 is a powerful verse that speaks to the unyielding devotion and unwavering faith of the psalmist towards God. This verse is a declaration of the psalmist's commitment to praising and glorifying God in every circumstance, whether good or bad. The psalmist acknowledges that God is worthy of all honor and praise, and that it is their duty as a believer to exalt His name.

The context of this verse is important to understand its significance. Psalm 34 is a psalm of David, written during a time when he was on the run from King Saul. David was in a difficult and dangerous situation, yet he remained faithful to God and trusted in His protection and provision. In the midst of his struggles, David wrote this psalm as a testimony to God's faithfulness and goodness.

In verse 1, David expresses his determination to bless the Lord at all times. This means that he will praise God not only when things are going well, but also in times of hardship and adversity. David recognizes that God is sovereign and in control of all things, and that He is worthy of praise regardless of the circumstances.

David also declares that God's praise shall continually be in his mouth. This means that he will not only praise God in his heart, but also with his words. David understands that our words have power, and that speaking words of praise and thanksgiving can change our perspective and lift our spirits.

Psalm 34:1 is a powerful declaration of faith and devotion to God. It reminds us that no matter what we are going through, we can always trust in God's goodness and faithfulness. As believers, we are called to bless the Lord at all times and to continually have His praise on our lips. May we always remember to honor and glorify God in every circumstance, for He is worthy of all praise and adoration.

Prayer:

Dear God, I come before You today with a heart full of gratitude and praise. I declare with confidence that I will bless You at all times, and Your praise shall continually be in my mouth. I thank You for Your unending love, grace, and mercy that sustain me through every season of life.

Lord, I acknowledge that You are sovereign and in control of all things. I trust in Your protection and provision, even in the midst of difficult circumstances. I pray that Your name would be exalted and glorified in my life, and that Your praise would continually be on my lips.

Help me to have a heart of gratitude and thanksgiving, even in the midst of trials and hardships. May Your love and faithfulness be a constant source of strength and comfort to me.

I pray this in the powerful name of Jesus, Amen.

EXTRA DAY THIRTY-ONE

"I beseech you therefore, brethren, by the mercies of God, that you present your bodies a living sacrifice, holy, acceptable to God, which is your reasonable service. 2 And do not be conformed to this world, but be transformed by the renewing of your mind, that you may prove what is that good and acceptable and perfect will of God." - Romans 12:1-2

Romans 12:1-2 is a powerful passage that emphasizes the importance of offering ourselves as living sacrifices to God.

The passage emphasizes that God is deserving of our worship and that we should offer ourselves as living sacrifices to Him. It is a call to recognize God's goodness and to respond with a heart of worship and adoration. The passage also emphasizes the importance of transformation and the renewing of our minds.

The phrase "by the mercies of God" emphasizes the importance of recognizing God's mercy and grace. It is a reminder that we are saved by grace through faith in Jesus Christ, and that our worship and service to God should be characterized by a spirit of gratitude and thanksgiving.

The phrase "present your bodies as a living sacrifice" emphasizes the importance of offering ourselves fully to God. It is a call to surrender our lives to Him and to live for His glory. It is a reminder that our worship should be characterized by a spirit of sacrifice and devotion.

The phrase "which is your spiritual worship" emphasizes the importance of worshiping God with our whole being. It is a reminder that worship is not just about singing songs or attending church, but about offering ourselves fully to God in every area of our lives.

The phrase "Do not be conformed to this world, but be transformed by the renewing of your minds" emphasizes the importance of transformation and the renewing of our minds. It is a call to reject the values of the world and to be transformed by the power of the Holy Spirit. It is a reminder that our thinking and behavior should be characterized by a spirit of holiness and obedience to God.

Romans 12:1-2 is a call to all believers to offer themselves as living sacrifices to God. It emphasizes the importance of recognizing God's goodness and responding with a heart of worship and adoration. It is a reminder that our worship should be characterized by a spirit of sacrifice and devotion, and that our thinking and behavior should be transformed by the power of the Holy Spirit.

Prayer:

Lord God, As I come before You today, I am filled with a heart of worship and adoration. I want to present my body as a living sacrifice, holy and acceptable to You, which is my spiritual worship. You are the Creator of the universe, the King of kings and Lord of lords, and the One who holds all power and authority. You are great and Your name is to be glorified.

Thank You, God, for Your mercy and grace. I am grateful for Your salvation and for the privilege of offering myself as a living sacrifice to You. Help me to remember Your goodness and to respond with a heart of worship and adoration.

As I offer myself to You, I ask that You would transform me by the renewing of my mind. Help me to reject the values of the world and to be transformed by the power of Your Holy Spirit. May my thinking and behavior be characterized by a spirit of holiness and obedience to You.

Lord, I pray that You would help me to live a life that is pleasing to You. May my words and thoughts be pleasing in Your sight, and may I honor You in all that I do. Help me to love and honor others as brothers and sisters in Christ, and to be patient in times of trouble.

Thank You, God, for the privilege of serving You. May all that I do bring honor and glory to Your name, and may my life be a living sacrifice, holy and pleasing to You.

In Jesus' name I pray,
Amen.

ABOUT THE AUTHOR

Rev. Dr. Dennis J Snyder is a retired pastor and biblical counselor. He was a Senior Pastor of churches in Indiana and Michigan for more than 35 years. Dennis has a BA in Pastoral Ministry/Religious Education, Masters in Theology, and a Doctorate in Theology with an emphasis in Biblical Counseling. He has been married to his lovely wife, Vicki, for 52 years. They have two children and five grandchildren. He enjoys fishing and golfing in his spare time.

More Books by Pastor Dennis Snyder

https://amzn.to/44ZnmLd 30 Day Devotional:Trust, Anxiety, and Hope

https://amzn.to/464AdfJ 30 Day Devotional: Righteousness and Holiness

https://amzn.to/3r2PT3v **12 Steps to A Healthy Marriage**

https://amzn.to/46lHMze **Biblical Discipleship: It's Importance in the Christian life**

https://amzn.to/42Vrc6r **The Book of Romans Study Questions**

https://amzn.to/3Xk2rji **Biblical Financial Management: Managing money God's Way**

Looking at Life Through the Grid of the Bible

A series of self-directed Bible Studies

Book one: Proof of Heaven: From the Bible not Near Death Experiences https://amzn.to/3Od0qT9

Book two: Angelology: The Study of Angels Good and Bad https://amzn.to/44IIEMR

Book three: Seven Deadly Sins https://amzn.to/3JXQaeK

Made in the USA
Middletown, DE
01 October 2023

39798030R00040